e l e v e n .

A Book of Gems

shaine amir

DEDICATION

This book is dedicated all my friends. I love my family too but my friends are the ones that I have spent the majority of my life with. You became my family at times when I didn't have any. You opened your homes at times where I had nowhere to go. No money left to spend. I would not be here without you. Thank you, for allowing me to be different from all of you but still very similar in many ways. You never questioned my individuality, only shed light on it. So, I hope this book is able to bring light to your darkest places. If they ever talk down on any of you, I will defend you. I love you all differently but the fact that there is love in the first place is what matters most. I pray for you on your best and worst days. I am in debt to all of you, for believing in my dreams.

And for my family, times were never 100 percent easy for us. The love didn't always seem evident and apparent but it was there. I appreciate you all because you helped shape me. You supported everything that I ever wanted to do in my life.

Thank you.

This is a cold world; these gems will help you stay cozy. Forever cozy.

CONTENTS

ACKNOWLEDGMENTS

A very special thanks goes out to some of my closest friends; Christopher, Crystal, Dante, and Huggs. Thank you for allowing me to complain. Thank you for educating me. Thank you for helping me with representation and presentation. Thank you for providing me the resources that I lacked. Thank you for the time, you will never get it back but I'm glad you spent it on me.

E l e v e n .

Gem /jem/ noun
1. A precious stone, especially when cut, polished or engraved.
2. You.

I've been scared to admit it but I have a lot of emotions that weigh heavy on my heart. No matter how emotional people label me, I will always be me. No matter how much people say that they feel where I'm coming from, they will never relate. It's the things I never speak on, that are doing the most damage to my soul. I've spent eleven months, attempting to heal the bruises left by family, lovers, and friends. For eleven months and four seasons, I fought battles of my own and of others. Lost tears and blood. But most importantly, in those eleven months, I lost myself. I became desensitized and couldn't decipher which love was real and which love would last.

Every single person in this world is a gem and your souls will shine as bright as you allow them to. For about a year now, I've shared all of my pain, love, and trauma with you all. I transformed tears into poetry and poetry into art. When all of the pain left, I thought that my words would too. But through everything I was able to create this masterpiece for you.

1

BE A WALLFLOWER

Wallflowers play dead. Wallflowers hear everything and know everything but play dumb, deaf and blind. Play dead. By playing dead, you are able to save energy that you didn't know you had. But remember to see everything. Watch how people move. And even if a situation pertains to you, that doesn't mean your reaction is required.

Allow people to mention your name. It only elevates your reputation. The people who know you for who you are, won't listen. While the people who don't know you—but want to, are tuning in. So, play deaf too, but hear everything. Then, when they come asking questions… wipe the coal out of your eyes. Play dumb, because being a fool is the best <u>in this</u> <u>case</u>. It'll show you how smart the individuals around you truly are.

This is important. In order to save yourself, train yourself to be like a wallflower. The loudest person in the room isn't always the "brokest". Most importantly, the loudest person in the room is not the one that is talking. In fact, it's the person who is silently observing... the wallflower.

The louder you are, the less chance you allow yourself to be a mystery. The more played out you become. It is in your best interest to always appear as mysterious as possible. The more you speak, the less knowledge you obtain.

Playing dead is the only way that we as humans can make ourselves invisible. Your presence does not always need to be announced. Put yourself on standby. Be present physically, but allow people to think that mentally, your mind is elsewhere. Making it always known that you are paying attention is not going to work in your favor. Teach yourself to blend in from time to time and you will be surprised at how much information you can gain. *Robert*

Greene teaches us to, "always say less than necessary," which is indeed true. Note that, "less", that Green refers to can also be nothing at all. You do not need to speak, in order to be heard.

You should play deaf too. This part is really tough. People will say whatever to test your patience but you can only react to what you hear. **You are the one that decides what you hear.** Words are used to deceive you, do not ever listen too deeply. Playing dumb puts, you in front of everyone else and they'll assume that you have no clue what is going on. They'll assume that you understand nothing. Then, when everything crumbles, they will understand why making assumptions is always the wrong route to take.

Those who are quiet and playing dumb, can be whoever they choose to be and hear everything that they need to hear. Never assume that you will elevate yourself by bragging about yourself. Also, never assume that you will elevate yourself by tearing other people down. You won't.

Wallflowers are that and exactly that. Flowers against the wall. This Gem is first because once you get this down, you will deplete the desire to always be seen, to be heard, or to be understood. We wallflowers do not crave, nor seek attention, though it may still find its way to us. Playing dead, deaf, and dumb will, "stir the pot". The men and women who live the longest are the ones who see everything and hear everything, but act dumber than they are. They do not need to make the intellect and information that their minds hold, known to others.

That is how a person survives the final round. Don't get me wrong, making it to the final round is cool… but the crowd never cheers for second place. With this one gem, you'll be able to acquire all the knowledge you want because you can then be whoever you choose to be.

2

STAY MUTUAL

Sides do not exist! Don't forget that. There's always side A, side B and side C. But remember, things come full circle. Those "sides" disappear. Do not take the time out to determine who's right. Someone is always right and often times, both people are right. So, do not try and determine which person is more correct than the other.

Only a fool chooses sides. Gatsby was a fool for Daisy. Do you remember how that ended? Remind yourself to always and I mean always, stay neutral. In order to understand a situation, we must look at it from three perspectives.

1. Your point of view.

2. The point of view of those involved.

3. A random person who has no ties to anyone at all.

It is not and never will be your job to choose sides. If you ever find yourself in the middle of a two-person argument, it is because you have chosen to stay there. Remove yourself from the toxins that are attempting to fill your soul.

As I stated previously, it may seem like there are two sides to a story but things always come full circle. So, there are actually no sides. Do not try and create any sides. Our ancestors fought for independence and the moment that we decide to choose sides, we give that up. However, committing to a person is different than choosing sides. Time will show you when and if you should ever commit.

People will hate you for not choosing their side. That is alright, I promise. The best leaders in this world were not loved. [1]Niccolo Machiavelli once said in his book, *The Prince,* *"It is better to be feared than loved."* **That is because those who base their relationships on love are often deceived.** Love is like any other emotion. It will grow or fade. Do not put your trust in what is temporary. I will not allow you to be deceived. Just because you love someone, does not make you obligated to run to their defense.

[2] *Aldous Huxley proclaims in his book, The Doors of Perception, "We live together, we act on and react to, one another but always in all circumstances we are by ourselves."*

---

[1] An Italian diplomat, politician, historian, philosopher, humanist and writer of the Renaissance period.

[2] Aldous Huxley is the author of the book, *The Doors of Perception.*

A wise man understands that there are never two sides, often times there are more. But the wisest man knows that it never ends well. Though we react off of other people's actions ad emotions, we are still by ourselves at the end of the day. Nobody is forcing you to take sides. And you won't ever take sides again because now you understand that there are **only circles and never squares. You lose the moment that you choose**; don't ever think that you're doing the noble thing by determining who is right and who is wrong.

3

APPEAR EMOTIONAL

Being too emotional will hinder you from understanding what's in front of you. Being emotional will hurt you. However, appearing emotional will cause people to run to you. Then, those people will tell you their stories… listen but be careful what you share. Remember, the moment you become emotional, is the moment that you lose.

You can either choose to think with your emotions or think logically. As stated, your emotions will hinder you from understanding exactly what is in front of you. When you are thinking emotionally, you are thinking with bias. You are incorporating your feelings, with your judgement of the person or the situation. It is hard, I know. As humans, feelings are natural. We can't always control how we feel but we can always control how we choose to express our emotions.

Thinking logically will allow you to understand the situation in its entirety. More importantly, you will no longer be making yourself a victim because you feel personally attacked. Thinking logically is a foundational skill that can help you at any stage of your life. It will improve the relationships with the people in your life. Believe it or not, logical thinking will improve your emotions, too.

You can and must appear as emotional as you need, in order to get the reactions and information that you want from other people. Be what they need you to be,

but stay who you are deep down. Come off as
emotional when attempting to learn about others.

An emotional response to any situation in your life will
only cause you temporary satisfaction. You will still be left to
analyze things afterwards. Take time if you need to and allow
your emotions to flee so that you can think freely, but logically
at the same time.

Play whatever role you need to in order to survive. When
you are emotional, it loosens the knots. People will be more
receptive and more expressive. For two reasons: Because you
are safe; and because you are a safe for them to store their
secrets, emotions, and problems at. This Gem is tough.

The moment that you become engulfed in your feelings,
what is going on in front of you begins to blur. Sometimes
people lose control because they have given into their
emotions. You will not.

4

SPEND TIME BY YOURSELF

Take as much time as you need to in order to understand yourself and who you are becoming. But do not be fooled—there's a difference. Never isolate yourself. As you grow and are becoming more eager to understand who you are, you'll need to converse. That will further your intellect.

Accept that you do not know it all. It is what you can take from others that will help you grow. Isolating yourself will cause a loss of support. Then, you will be forgotten about. Isolation is never the answer, it burns bridges.

Things come in three's, never pairs. Which means, there will be people who you know that will understand your desire for isolation. There will be people who know you and won't understand your reasoning for isolation. Lastly, there will be people you have never met because you've chosen to isolate yourself. You can be around others while you are still trying to see who you are and what you like. Think of it as taste testing. You need to try different things in order to be sure of your interest.

Spend time by yourself so that you are accustomed to it, should you ever have no one in your corner. Babies are dependent. Do not be a baby. We've grown past that. Spend time by yourself because if you do not understand yourself, someone will come along and try to build up a version of you that they want you to be. Do not allow that. We as humans crave intimacy from other people. We crave acceptance and we never know exactly what it is that we want people to accept. Understand who you are. Accept who you are. And never forget it. [3]*Robert Greene* teaches us that isolation is dangerous and this is true because we never want to disconnect ourselves from the world. We want to be able to participate in it, rather than cutting ourselves off from valuable information.

Do not allow life to pass you by. You will end up missing out on everything you didn't know was possible for you. Cutting ties with people is beneficial, but cutting ties with EVERYONE is not.

---

[3] Robert Greene is the author of *48 Laws Of Power.*

5

THE PRESSURE
OF
SECOND CHANCES

The ball is in your court now, and it will be forever. Remember, in life it is always best for you to receive a second chance, never to give one. Should you ever receive a second chance and all fails, the other person will always lose more than you.

Gem number 5 takes a bit of a twist. You are given several gems in one. This specific gem will teach you; how to have power over others, how to abuse that power and most importantly it teaches you, how you can potentially lose the power that you have over others. Do not allow one to have the opportunity to make you look dumber than you are.

When receiving a second chance the power is given to you because that person(s) has submitted to you. You have been deemed worthy to them. You can control the person and the situation. Show the person different sides of you so that they think you've changed. **But never change** if you are given a second chance. People give second chances when they are looking for changed personality. Remind yourself who it was that this person wanted you to be. Then, become that person, to get everything that you want. Use words and action equally.

Both the receiver and the giver have the ability to abuse their power. The receiver must understand that it is all mental. Train yourself to pick at the mind of the person who has given you a second chance. They may not be weak, **but** they have a weak spot for you. Use it to your advantage. For some reason, you were worth the second chance. Remember that.

You'll only lose a friend or an opportunity, should you receive a second chance and things do not work out. You can make more friends and you will create more opportunities for yourself as life progresses. All of the time that the other person has invested in you and your potential, cannot be earned back. We can never make up for lost time.

To the ones that are giving out the second chances, understand I am not telling you that you shouldn't. But remember that time is the most important, non-tangible item, that we as humans choose to waste. Choose how much time you waste and with whom you waste it with, carefully.

shaine amir

6

ACCEPT YOUR PAST

Move forward with the people who are walking that way. Only help those with the desire to progress. Embracing people from your past once you have stepped into your future is dangerous. You are giving the impression that even though you have moved on, you have come back for them because you have time for them. You don't have time. Let others play catch up.

You should always pay it forward and help those on the rise. But you must remember that not all people deserve your help. Just because you may have; more experience, more knowledge, and more wisdom to share to those younger than you, does not mean that they are ready for it. Some people are not moving in the same direction as you. Do not make the assumption that people want to follow the same path as you either. More importantly, do not assume that people have even determined what path they want to travel. Some people are still finding themselves.

Now that we have situated them, let's talk about you. The future can be scary if you are not fully sure of what is next for you or how you will get there. It doesn't mean that you should fall straight back into old habits. In order to fail, you have to try something new. Forget about what you're used to, what you did back then, and how it made you feel. Become comfortable being uncomfortable. Your future involves new jobs, new activities, new friends, and new partners. Do not look back—you are where you are for a reason.

Every job is not going to be the same. You may be the manager at one place and at the next one, you may be getting managed. These things are reminders that nothing is permanent and that you must know what every level is like before you figure out which level you want to be at for sure. Should you ever be demoted from any position, remember the way you felt when you think about giving up. It's okay to be unhappy with where you are, but don't look back. Figure out how to make the best out of whatever situation you are currently in and think about how you can do better than the last time you were, "at your best".

Not everyone deserves second chances but you know that by now. Relationships can be hard to deal with and it can be hard to get over someone, true. But be careful stepping back into your past. It is okay to reminisce. Understand that just because your mind thinks of people from your past, does not mean that you need to run to people from your past.

People are in your past for a reason. Your new relationships won't necessarily be anything like the last and you may become hesitant. Different is good, it is great. Never assume that you are doing yourself a favor, by staying in your comfort zone. Allow your personality to grow. Cherish the memories and move on.

This gem stands for platonic relationships as well. It's okay to cry about your previous mistakes, tell stories from your past, and even reminisce but never go backwards. Do not assume that your friends are growing with you. They may not be and that's okay too. Just know that it is not your job to create a path for them to follow. Do not allow people to lean on your success. People will eat with you, as if they have starved with you. People are only able to flourish because you have kept them around, though they are of no benefit to you.

It's okay to have people dependent on you but make sure that whatever you give to them, you have given yourself first. Do not always feel the need to be available for those in your past. People come back when they see you are doing well.

People will leech off of your success and others will talk down

on where you are. Tell them to catch up because now that you

have this gem, you are leading the way.

7

NEVER FORGIVE

People do not change and that is fine. Accept
it and move on. People only show you the sides of
them that they want you to see. The sides of
them that they had all along. Just because you
have not forgiven, doesn't mean that you are,
"still hurt". You are just aware. Actions deserve
forgiveness. Not personality traits.

People never change. Thus, why bother forgiving people for who they are? People show you who they are and at all times, people are who they choose to be. If we want to grow as individuals, we must accept that and move forward.

People will make assumptions once they are not forgiven by a person. They will assume that they haven't done enough. They will assume that you are still mad or hurt. They may get the idea in their heads that you are planning to get even. Allow them to think whatever they want. You do not owe people explanations on how you chose to act. You can decide who you choose to forgive and not forgive. Do not be mad at a person for being shy, that is them, it is a part of their personality. However, you have every right to be upset at the actions they take, because people know the personality traits that they possess.

In, *The Four Agreements,* [4]**Don Miguel Ruiz teaches us that making assumptions only creates more lies and misunderstandings.** Train yourself to ask questions when and

---

[4] Don Miguel Ruiz is the author of *The Four Agreements.*

if you should ever be uncertain of something. Communicate clearly, that way all misconceptions are avoided. One should never assume, even if they believe it is something they know. Making assumptions will create gossip and rumors.

Assumptions and rumors will lead to fights. Fights will lead to war. Try to avoid going to war. Just because someone has told you something does not mean that it is true. Never assume that anything is happening because of you. People will act in their own ways, whether you do anything or not.

Lastly, just because you have not forgiven someone for what they have done does not mean that you are holding grudges. You must simply accept what happened and move on. You must understand that their role in your life has changed because you have learned more about who that person truly is. Just be cordial and you will be fine.

8

DO NOT HOLD GRUDGES

Grudges will only hurt you. I promise. All grudges do is force you to be angry with a person, over a situation that has happened already. Let me tell you, people notice. They always do. So, no need to hold grudges—hold on to memories and go forward.

A grudge implies that there is a nonstop feeling of resentment towards an action or person. This is different from not forgiving. Forgive people for what they have done if it has hurt you but accept that it has determined who they are. People are determined by what they do, not by what they say they will do or are capable of doing. Although you may feel pain, do not allow it to sit on your heart or your mind. It will do you no good. You are forcing yourself to indirectly reminisce about the traumas in your life.

There are three actions that must take place:

1. Understand that it is okay to cry.

2. Put first things first.

3. Accept that you are hurt and understand that you will heal.

I'm almost certain that your parents have told you that, "you're never too old to be beaten," mine did. Do not ever feel like you are too old to cry either. You're never too old to feel pain. Crying when you need to is the first step in becoming the master of your emotions, rather than building walls. **The more walls you build, the less you are able to express how you feel.** Don't become that person who can no longer communicate what is on their heart and mind. So yes, **cry if you need to**, men and women. Nobody is excluded and despite the social constructs... nobody was ever excluded.

Stephen R. Covey [5] is the author of the notable book, "*The 7 Habits of Highly Effective People*". One habit this book teaches is for us to always, "*Put first things first*". Covey's book teaches you how to balance your personal and professional life. The two should never mix or get in the way of one another. There will always be time for love; never let it affect you once you step into your office. At every age, people are learning about themselves and trying to figure themselves out.

Work on the things that are not urgent and important, just as you work on the things that are urgent and important.

---

[5] Stephen R. Covey is the author of, *The 7 Habits of Highly Effective People*.

Remind yourself that these are the things that are contributing to your future and how you will end up. Grudges will hold you back and cause you to do nothing more but waste your time on something that is neither important, nor urgent.

Focus on everything that you need and put what you want, to the side. A broken heart will heal. Chase your dreams. Even with all the time on your hands, do not assume that time is on your side. Become proactive, establish routines and use the pain to rebuild yourself. This will help you remove the resentment that you have. The busier you make yourself, the more you will forget the pain you feel. It is okay to want things, and your life will make time for the things that you want.

Waste the extra time on things that you want but spend precious time on the things that you need. That means… only in your free time and only after you have cleared your checklist… should there be time for fun or to even pay attention the people you have problems with.

Most importantly, you must still acknowledge that you are hurt. It is okay to be hurt. **Living in denial does nothing, lying to people about your pain, does nothing**. You are only hurting yourself when you lie to others that are checking on your mental and physical well-being, by telling them that you are okay. You will end up sending away those who can help you heal.

Everyone has gone through the healing process before. People do not like to acknowledge the pain that they feel because they fear that it will make them seem weak. If that's the case, then what does lying to yourself make you? A liar.

Pick your poison. Lying to the ones we love sounds warmhearted and caring, but it's never something that we should do. Lying to yourself however, is a different conversation. How can you mend the sores on your heart and the holes in your soul if you cannot even acknowledge that they are there? By lying to yourself about the problems that are still encompassing your heart, you allow the pain to fester and grow.

Do not underestimate how far conversations with people can go. Sometimes we need to speak to other people to get a different perspective from the ones that we've been given. Sometimes we need to speak to people about what we are going through because they may have been there before. Do not assume that you can look at someone and tell that they have not gone through what you have gone through.

Hold grudges if you choose. They may not notice, but your heart will. You are hurting yourself. Accept that people change and know that you must learn to adjust and act accordingly.

9

TIME SECURES NO BOND
&
TITLES ENSURE NO LOYALTY

It does not matter how long you have been together for. Your partner will leave you in the blink of an eye. You may not believe that relationships work that way, which is okay. But that is how people work, you see. At the same time, understand that a bond that has felt like a lifetime, can be formed in a day.

Please don't think that the amount of time spent together matters. It does not matter now and it won't matter in the long run; this is not meant to be depressing. People wake up with different feelings every day. That is why we must never put too much trust in the ones who are the closest to us.

We must learn to use those who stand at a distance. The great author, Robert Greene [6] teaches us that to **never commit to anyone**. That will get you in more trouble than you believe. Always choose yourself. People assume that because they have known their best friends since they were in kindergarten that things won't change between them.

How long you have known someone means nothing.
How long you have known someone means nothing.
How long you have known someone means nothing.

The truth is that time secures no relationships or friendships. Relationships are jobs, yes. But relationships do not come with pensions. Nothing is

[6] Robert Greene is the author for *48 Laws of Power.*

guaranteed; happiness, love, fidelity, nothing. Titles mean nothing at all and as hard as it may seem for people to accept, they never will mean anything. People see titles and they input value. "Oh, this is her husband and they have kids. She's so lucky." Remember, we can't make that assumption. She may very well be dying inside, as could he. Some people stay because the time spent together makes them feel like they must. Everyone that seems to be placed in a happy position is not always happy. Everyone who seems to be at their lowest point is not always.

Titles are nothing more than words. Words are used to deceive you.

Titles are nothing more than words. Words are used to deceive you.

Titles are nothing more than words. Words are used to deceive you.

The real value is and always will be placed in the actions that people take for you. Never the titles that people make for you. If titles solidified anything, then the term, "ex" would not be existent. Divorce papers would not be getting signed on a daily basis. I'm not saying this to be pessimistic, I just want you to know... incase nobody else told you any of this. Even if they post your photos on social media, that means nothing. Social media is a world that creates problems because they don't have to deal with them.

Have marriages not proven that nothing in this world is secure or permanent? Do not rely on titles. People will love you more than the ones they have married and trust you more than the ones they've spent every moment with. **It is about who has the secrets. It's about who understands the dark moments and it will NEVER be about who was there first.**

You know that you've heard it before... Even your family will treat you like the strangers that they pass on the street. They don't care about the fact that you share the same blood. They'll watch you bleed out if they feel like it. Family is family and blood is blood. But when it's all said and done, that means nothing. Sometimes, the ones who carried you in their stomach, will act like they grabbed you from the trash.

Family will forget that you never asked to be here, when you ask them for help. That's what people do, they act selfishly when they choose to, family or not. The family cuts/wounds hurt the most and take the longest to heal because you both share the same DNA. They'll always know exactly what places to hit when they go to hurt you.

Don't let these titles fool you. Often time's people are never labeling/providing titles to the ones who are truly close to them. Those are the ones that are protected and out of harm's way. Things like titles allow people to believe that everyone is living up to them and that's not always going to be true.

Friends for long doesn't mean friends for life.

10

THERE MUST BE "THEM" IN ORDER FOR THERE TO BE "US"

It is okay to be separated from the bunch. If everyone was the same, then who you are would mean nothing. Embrace the fact that you have been given stripes to wear, amongst those in solid colored clothing.

There is no reason to ever want to fit in. Let that sink in. Accepting your indifference to certain things is indeed a growing pain. It teaches you to cherish your individuality. Individualistic minds are inclined to solitude. As your mind grows, not everyone who used to understand you will understand you.

It's a weird feeling at first, to be in a room full of people that you know, and to still feel alone. *I know, I know.* It's never about the capacity of the room. It's just about you not understanding why you don't fit in. Understand who you are becoming by understanding what it is you don't like. By understanding what you don't want to be like. By understanding who you don't want to be like.

Know that should you choose to go your whole life "fitting in", that isn't living. That is just existing. Before you die, you better try and see what it's like to actually live. It is not and never will be a problem that you do not breathe like "them". It is not a problem that poetry and art is what moves your heart. Don't look for everything to make sense in your life. And know that everything won't always make sense, especially if you are comparing your life to others.

Joanne Green[7], once said, "take time and in due time, time will come". Live by this. Only a fool rushes, so do not be that fool. Give yourself time. Allow yourself to step into unknown territory. Become comfortable with being uncomfortable. Allow the new phases and transitions in your life to happen to you and then adjust to them. Never move hastily. You are sure to miss things that way.

I AM GIVING YOU GEMS.

Aldous Huxley [8] is one of the most notable British authors of the all-time. In his final book, *Island,* published in 1962 he said, "***It's dark because you are trying too hard. Lightly child, lightly. Learn to do everything lightly. Yes, feel lightly even though you're feeling deeply.***
Just lightly let things happen and lightly cope with them".

---

[7] Joanne Green. December 20th, 2017. Personal Communication.

[8] Aldous Huxley is the author of the 1962 novel *Island.*

Understanding who you are can be challenging. Growth is one of the hardest things in life because we have to train ourselves to accept that we are growing away from people we know and shedding parts of the person we once were. However, never make situations dark. Find the light within them. Do not try too hard to make sense of things and do not try too hard to understand why you are not like them. Moving "lightly" requires that you never overthink or think too deeply about what is going on. Sometimes you must embrace it all while it is happening and understand that it is a new chapter in your life. Do not force your mind to understand immediately, you are sure to cause yourself headaches.

They laughed at Waldo but they never forgot who he was. **Let them make up rumors, conspiracies, and side group chats about you but then come smile in your face.** It is okay to be different because you will be sure to leave your mark. I promise. It will take some time but you will be fine.

eleven.

11

WHAT YOU DO WHEN YOU'RE HAPPY AND HEALTHY, MEANS NOTHING

Show us how you move when you are wounded.

When you are hardest hit is when your work is

worth the most. Everyone isn't expecting you to

push through. And then, just when everyone has

counted you out, you hit the corner and cross the

finish line before anyone else.

As many people as there are cheering for you, know that there are the same amount of people praying that you lose. You have to be twice as good to even be mentioned, don't forget that. What you do when you're happy and healthy means nothing in comparison to what you do when you're hurt. Don Miguel Ruiz[4] teaches us that we must always do our best.

He reminds us that our "best" is definitely subject to change over time. The best that we can do when we are healthy, is not the same that we can do when we are unhealthy. Yes, we know that. Now, in the presence of mercy, remind yourself that nobody is expecting you to win. Everyone is expecting you to lose. In the presence of mercy, remind yourself that all pain is temporary. All emotions are temporary.

When you are happy and healthy excuses do not exist. When you are not happy and healthy, excuses are expected. Do not be predictable, do not be what's expected. It is when your back is against the wall and all you have to look at are the bricks and cement... that you will truly see, just how strong you are. This is a gem.

Show them that you can work when you are bruised. Do not work yourself to death but train yourself to not accept pain. Pain does not last, it is mental. You're expected to excel when you are in perfect condition. But it's when you're hardest hit and the world's shown you all signs of failure instead of success, that you must prove yourself. Your back can be against the wall, that's fine but turn around and create a tunnel out of there.

Hidden Gems

Sometimes you have to kill who you are in order to become who you want to be. You have to kill who you are, in order to become who you are destined to be. Accept who you are but always want more for yourself. Don't settle. First, you must believe that you exist. Acknowledge that you exist and then start living your life. These eleven gems paint scenarios, allow for self-reflection and reveal emotionless filled lessons.

Understand that in every moment of your life, you are building memories. Memories last forever, people and moments do not. Don't get caught up in the moment or the people. They change, but the memories never do.

Nobody and nothing, will ever be, "out of your league". Leagues do not exist. Anything you want, you can have. Second guessing is a mind killer. Attack confidently and boldly. Do not create things that do not exist. All that does is provide you a false reality. Create your own reality with the things that do exist.

Be extraordinary. Being ordinary is… well, it's ordinary. Life is too short to be basic.

Master your emotions. What you do not say, your body language will show. Body language is the biggest part of our emotions.

Understand that you are everything you will ever need and you always will be.

Remember, in case you skipped this part… Though time is infinite, it can still run out on you, don't waste it.

The longer you put conversations off for, the more they will fester in your mind, body, and soul.

Youth is not immortality.

eleven.

INDEX

1. Ruiz, D. M. (1997). *The Four Agreements: A Practical Guide to Personal Freedom*. Amber-Allen Pub.

2. Huxley, A. (1962). *Island*.

3. Huxley, A. (1954). *The Doors of Perception*. Harper and Rowe.

4. Covey, S. R. (1989). *7 Habits of Highly Effective People*. Simon & Schuster ltd.

5. Greene, R. (1998). *The 48 Laws of Power*. Viking Press.

6. Green. J (2017). Personal Communication.

7. Machiavelli, N. (1532). *The Prince.*

ABOUT THE AUTHOR

Shaine Amir is a 21-year-old young male from Brooklyn, NY. A current graduate student at the University at Albany, SUNY. The gems were written by him but for everyone else going through the motions of life. On his social media pages, Shaine Amir shares his success, his poetry, and his business with the world. Through these platforms you can purchase framed pieces of his poems and order personalized poems for yourself.

INSTAGRAM: @WORDSBYAMIR //
@SHAINEPAGNEPAPI

TWITTER: @SHAINEAMIR

THINGS AND SUCH

<u>Sit down, I have wine for you</u>

I never wanted to get to know you. I wanted to watch
you from afar. So, I could see all the cracks, pen marks,
stumbles and falls. I wish I just stayed invisible and
never spoke up. I wish I stayed dreaming about you and
never woke up. Because to be honest, to be quite honest.
I'm more so in love with the person I thought you were.
But now you know me and you understand that I don't
breathe how you believed I did. You get to see that my
language is poetry and you see all my introverted ways.
You understand that trap music doesn't move me, like
the sounds of spoken word. I wish I could go back to
watching from afar. Keep that same old idea. Of me.
Don't get me wrong, the times we've talked, I've been
amazed at the contrast between who I thought you were
and who you are. There was just something more
interesting about watching you from afar. But since
you're here, why not let you in my world. Come.

Sit down, I have wine for you.

Send a thank you letter.

Your man should thank me. Not for the earrings that you still wear when he takes you to dinner. Not for the perfume I gave you that marinates in his clothes. Not for his favorite movie, that is yours because it is mine. He should thank me that he has you. I was the   sacrificial lamb, on your road to discovery. Countless nights, I allowed you to sample the beds of multiple men, ruining the home we were trying to build. I'm the reason for your mansion with him, don't you know? I gave up so many parts of me, loss so much sleep, shed so many tears, just for you to grow. So yes, your man should thank me and I feel that it's about time he knows. When your lips kiss his and after he tucks you in. Make sure that he goes to the night stand and writes a "thank you" letter in black pen. The truth is, I don't even want you back; he can have you and you can have him. But I think that some thanks are in order and homage must be showed. For all those nights that you did what you did and then came home. Let it be known, I never lost you. You were just too stupid to see that you were lucky to have me, I was your horseshoe. I taught you everything that makes his heart melt. Tell him send my thank you letter in black ink and make sure it's heartfelt.

Dear Men,

We have the right to feel pain. And fill that pain with tears. I pray that you never let your male ego change the way you live. Just remember, that when people no longer cry for you, you'll have to cry for yourself. And remember, all that money and wealth, could never fix up your mental health. How are you going to grow, if things are not right at home? Listen to your problems and take care of your heart. Take care of all the pieces of you, that have fallen apart. Take care. There is a social construct that has been bestowed upon us, stating that men can't be emotional. Allow me step forth first for us. For the one's afraid to talk about it, I'll take the microphone on your behalf. For the one's labeled "too emotional", don't blame yourself for letting them get too close to you. And for the ones who can't cry anymore I feel your pain. Leave the pain in the rear view. Create your own aesthetic of man. Before you allow someone to contribute to the breaking of you. Make sure that you contribute to the process of making you. For the men.

Dear Men.

Dear Women,

I apologize on behalf of the men who shower you in
gold, not knowing that you are made of that.
On behalf of the men who attempt to degrade you, not
understanding they didn't make you.
The day that men understand you are more than sexual
satisfaction, is the day they'll deserve a fraction.
Of you.
A rose, the most beautiful.
Dear women, I pray you stop giving the same apologies.
To the men who do not understand the definition of
misogyny.
Dear women, I apologize for the ones who've treated
you like you were a game of Tetris.
Do not allow them to build you up and break you down.
You are golden, with or without your crown.
For all of the one's who said you weren't worth their
stay.
Here are words of inspiration, for you to stick around
another day.
Dear. Women.

REST IN PEACE JOCELYN REED.

Made in the USA
Middletown, DE
23 September 2020

20465670R00042